DEALING WITH MENTAL ILLNESS
BOOK TWO
STRESS AND PTSD

DEALING WITH MENTAL ILLNESS BOOK 2

First edition. July 10, 2017.

Copyright © 2017 Rodney C. Cannon and Leo Hardy.

Written by Rodney C. Cannon and Leo Hardy.

STRESS
By.
Rodney C. Cannon

CHAPTER ONE STRESS AND YOUR HEALTH

-The number one root of all illness, as we know, is stress. - Marianne Williamson

Most people know chronic or overwhelming stress affects their minds. What you may not know is how stress can also affect your body. If it is not appropriately dealt with, stress can kill you. When you learn about the relationship between stress and your physical health, you can make changes in your life to reduce stress, or seek help from your doctor.

What Is Stress?

When people think of stress, they think of the factors that cause it. You may have plenty to worry about in your everyday life. Perhaps you worry about your job, family, finances, or the future. You or a loved one may have serious concerns, such as health, a failing marriage, or money problems.

However, it is the way your body responds to stress that is the real problem. Whether you are stressed over a specific situation or are coping with ongoing stress, your body produces stress hormones. When you experience fear, anger, or anxiety, the stress hormones that are meant to alert you to danger can actually endanger your physical health.

Stress And Your Immune System

Your immune system is responsible for protecting you from disease. A strong, healthy immune system can detect harmful pathogens, and distinguish these agents from your body's healthy, normal tissues. A strong immune system is your body's best defense against many health issues, ranging from cancer and rheumatoid arthritis to the common cold.

The effects of stress on your immune system can cause serious complications. Chronic stress can undermine your immune system so it does not work effectively. When your immune system is weakened by stress, you have a higher risk of developing health and medical problems.

Stress And Weight Control

When you maintain your ideal weight, it reduces your risk of health issues. Diabetes, heart conditions, and some cancers are some of the conditions associated with obesity.

The hormone imbalance caused by chronic stress can interfere with your ability to control your weight. Ongoing stress can result in excess body fat and pounds. You may find it extremely difficult to lose weight, even if you diet and exercise regularly.

When stress results in belly fat, it can increase your risk of other serious conditions. As belly fat affects your internal organs, visceral fat can endanger your pancreas, kidneys, liver, and heart. Visceral fat can cause your arteries and colon to become inflamed. It also releases toxins into your bloodstream.

Stress And Your Digestive System

If you experience frequent constipation, diarrhea, gas, or bloating, stress could be the reason. While these issues can be uncomfortable, they are also unhealthy. If you are often constipated, harmful toxins can remain in your body. If you have persistent diarrhea, your body may not be absorbing the nutrition it needs to stay healthy.

Stress And Your Cardiovascular System

When you are experiencing a great deal of stress, your blood pressure increases. Your blood doesn't clot normally. The stress hormones themselves are harmful to your heart.

With these effects, chronic stress can increase your risk of a heart attack.

Stress And Brain Function

There is more to your brain than your mental health. The cortisol produced with long-term chronic stress can damage and even kill the brain's cells. Reduced cognitive function and memory loss can result.

Some studies suggest chronic stress can increase the risk of Alzheimer's disease and dementia. A healthy brain in the future can depend on reducing the stress in your life today.

Stress And Your Sleep Habits

A full night of restful sleep each night is important for good health. If you are worried and stressed, restful sleep may not be possible. You may awaken periodically throughout the night, not be able to fall asleep at all, or sleep too much to escape your worries. All of these habits affect your hormones, and can affect your general health.

Stress And Bone Health

High levels of cortisol from chronic stress can cause bone loss. When your bone density is decreased, you may develop osteoporosis. While osteoporosis is often thought to affect elderly persons and women, younger individuals and men can develop it, too.

Bones that are weak and thin increase your risk of fractures. If you do break a bone during a slip and fall accident, healing can be a slower process.

Stress And Your Body

Stress can affect every system and organ in your body. You may have trouble breathing, your muscles may be tensed, and you may develop headaches. Stress affects your musculoskeletal system, your respiratory system, your nervous system, and even your reproductive system. Health issues associated with chronic stress can range from minor issues to long-term complications, and even death.

Stress And Your Health

Stress does not need to cause illness, disease, or shorten your lifespan. You can take constructive action to stay healthy.

While it is impossible to eliminate every stress factor from your life, do what you reasonably can to avoid stress. You will find some factors that can be eliminated.

You can learn techniques to reduce the effects of stress, too. There are many options from which to choose. Some examples include practicing yoga, other forms of moderate exercise, enjoying a warm bath, and reading a book. Find an activity that helps you relax, and do it every day.

If you are overwhelmed by stress, and stress-reduction techniques do not help, consult with your doctor. You should never be embarrassed to make an appointment with your physician and ask for help. Your personal physician is familiar with your health history, and can recommend lifestyle changes or other methods to help you deal with stress. He will know the best approach for your particular situation. Cooperating with your doctor can be the first step to better health.

Stress can cause depression, anxiety, and feelings of helplessness and hopelessness. It can cause minor medical issues, and conditions that could be fatal. However, you do not have to live with chronic stress when help is available. Not only is a stress-free life much more enjoyable, it is also much healthier. You will definitely appreciate the benefits when stress no longer rules your life.

CHAPTER TWO THE CAUSES OF STRESS

- If you don't think your anxiety, depression, sadness and stress impact your physical health, think again. All of these emotions trigger chemical reactions in your body, which can lead to inflammation and a weakened immune system. Learn how to cope, sweet friend. There will always be dark days. -Kris Carr

These days stress seems to be an increasing problem for people in societies. If not dealt with stress can seriously affect mental and physical health, harming the emotional well-being of people that seem unable to cope with too much of it.

Here are the top causes of stress and tips on how to cope with them.

Health

The state of people's health can be a cause of stress for a variety of reasons. People begin to feel stressed if they believe that there is something wrong with their health. Been uncertain about health is not good for stress levels. Instead of worrying about may or may not be wrong get a diagnosis from a medical professional. A medical diagnosis will either remove stress as nothing is wrong, the treatment is likely to succeed, or that the condition can be controlled.

Stress can be coped with by quickly putting all required treatments into place.

Illness

Closely linked to health, illness is also a major cause of stress. Getting an illness means that people start to think about what it will take to recover, or even if recovery is possible. Often it is the unknown aspects of having an illness, which raise stress levels higher and higher. However depending upon the types of illness people are going through the amount of stress they endure can remain consistently high, or it can vary.

It some respects the stress from physical illnesses is easier to cope with than illnesses caused by, or related to mental health issues. To a certain extent physical illnesses are easier to cope with, as effective treatments or at least pain relief is more likely to be available. With physical illnesses beginning treatments will often allow you to cope with the stress better. Operations, drugs, physiotherapy as well as pain relief may assist people in dealing with stress.

When it comes down to dealing with the stress linked to mental health illnesses the issues can often be complicated. People need to develop their own ways with coping with stress. Many people benefit from talking to others such as family and friends, or counselors. Others may take longer to ask for help, though they may need that time to realize the full extent of their illness. In the short term taking medication may help reduce stress yet should not continued for long to avoid addiction to antidepressants.

Money

Issues revolving money are a major source of stress, which in turn leads to physical or mental health issues if ways to cope with it are not attempted, or successful. For the great majority of people that are stressed by money the basic problem is not having enough of it. High levels of debt and not having enough income to cover all repayments can be particularly stressful. Furthermore the threat of bankruptcy or foreclosure can drive people over the edge.

The best way of coping with money related stress is for people to seek help as quickly as possible. People who contact their creditors are more likely to rearrange their payments and worry less about losing businesses or properties.

Finance

Just like a lack of money, financial concerns cause major stress and anxiety. Finance problems include bad credit scores, failure to get a mortgage or business loans. Poor credit history can prevent from taking out low cost loans or affording insurance policies.

It is possible to cope with financially related stress by seeking out expert advice. Steps to improve credit ratings and to reach agreement with creditors can make things better.

CHAPTER THREE MANAGING STRESS

- Unprecedented financial pressures, and an ever-increasingly aggressive public culture, along with social, moral and spiritual fragmentation, are leading to lives being overwhelmed by stress, intolerable interior isolation and even quiet despair. - Sean Brady

Introduction

Experiencing stress in today's world is bound to happen no matter what a person does. How stressed you let yourself become however depend on how stressed you become and how often such a thing happens. These at least are the factors that you can have the greatest influence over. Stress can wear you out before your day ever begins, and can impact your physical and mental health alike. So the question is: what can you do? There are a vast number of methods and techniques that have been devised by hundreds of individuals who are considered experts in various fields of study and just as many disciplines. Listed below are just a few ideas that might help you to lead a less stressful existence. The main focus will always be on preventing stress from occurring in the first place, but this is also meant to grant you a few ideas of what to do when the inevitable happens and stress becomes a part of your daily life once again. There are many useful techniques and habits you can get into to reduce your stress levels, and all of them are designed at calming yourself and learning how to deal with the stress without becoming overwhelmed by it. So with that in mind, let's get right into it.

Effective Steps and Stress Management

1) Take on one thing at a time.

The less you have on your plate, metaphorically speaking, the more calm and composed you will be. It doesn't matter if it's work, school, or in your private life, taking on too much all at once can be a stressful experience that can seriously affect your health. Many people have developed the habit of attempting to multitask when it comes to life in order to save themselves a few extra minutes here and there. While this skill is quite impressive it can be harmful when taken to unhealthy extremes. Take things as they come, focus on finishing that one thing with a higher level of quality instead of having to redo something over and over again because you were stressed out when you did it the first time.

2) Document everything. Some people can benefit from a photographic or eidetic memory and can remember things picture perfect. For those who can't do this it is recommended to jot down notes or write down a brief blurb to remind yourself of the necessary information later on. Whether it's an idea, an important time or date, writing it down will eliminate the stress of having to remember or recreate the moment you spoke to someone or tried to memorize this or that fact that has suddenly eluded you. It is also possible that writing things down will help to increase your memory and allow you to recall far more than before, as repetitively writing notes down can help jog the mind in a much healthier manner.

3) Let small issues remain small. Trying to overthink a problem or an issue at hand usually makes matters worse and forces an individual to stress over something that might need the extra level of thought they give to it. By doing this you are essentially "making a mountain out of a molehill". When this occurs the mundane often becomes far more important than it might have otherwise been had you stopped to really think about the matter. It pays to take time to back up a bit and think on how important the issue truly is, and then decide whether or not it requires the extra thought and effort. In other words think first, think twice, and then deal with the issue that exists, not the one you could possibly create. In this way you can simplify the problem and find a much easier way to resolve it.

4) Don't guess, ask. If you don't know something or need to understand something or someone better then ask. Reading minds is

hard unless you know how to read body language and nonverbal signals, and even then, this method is not perfect. Communicate and avoid unnecessary conflicts, it will save a great deal of time and facilitate better interpersonal relations. There is no shame in asking for help when it is needed or in asking another person if you are unable to recall something important.

5) When the weekend arrives, disconnect. When the weekend comes, the balance between work and your personal life needs to be observed with a clear and distinct feel that leaves no question that you are on break and not at all available. Leave the cell phone, don't use the email, and let things ride until Monday. This is a hard task for many busybodies that need to be on call most times, but whenever possible, it is absolutely necessary to kick back and let your body and mind just zone out and relax. Human beings are not meant to operate at full capacity every single hour of the day, but too many people do attempt to do this and as a result suffer a very high risk of burnout in their career, schooling, or other venues. By taking the time to relax you can enjoy life a little more, keep your mind fluid and more capable of adapting to the surrounding environment, and most important, reduce your stress level.

Conclusion

Stress will always be a part of normal life, but there is positive stress and there is negative stress. The goal should always be to eliminate any negative stressors or at the very least minimize their effects on your overall health. By taking a few minutes each day to simply slow down, relax, and take a few deep breaths you will find that you can enjoy your day just a little more. Decreasing the amount of stress in your day can make you feel better and react better to your environment, and it will improve your physical health as well. Take a few moments each day to just breathe, relax, and let the stress just roll off of your shoulders.

CHAPTER FOUR STRESS ON THE BRAIN

- Stress is something that is sort of out of your control. You get stressed out over looking at the finish line. Stress is something that is an outside thing. Stress is an anxiety. - Joe Torre

When the human brain undergoes stress specific areas of the brain and body respond. We have developed a very specialized set of reactions when we perceive threats to our well-being or the safety of others. Fear of harm is a nearly universal stress trigger, but other events and expectations also cause stress for individuals, depending on personality and level of importance of these stressors. Prior experience with a variety of challenges also informs the brain as to whether an incident, encounter, or occurrence feels stressful.

Brain Sectors Affected

When the brain identifies a safety threat or a grave concern it sends a signal along the spinal cord to the adrenal glands. The adrenal glands answer by releasing adrenaline, a hormone that causes a number of bodily functions intended to prepare for protective action. Adrenaline acts by increasing blood sugar levels and heart rate and also raises blood pressure. A surge of energy flood the body due to these factors. Another hormone, norepinephrine, joins the adrenaline to help hyper-focus on the threat. Both of these hormones arouse the body to either "flight or fight" in response to the stressful event.

The amygdala, another part of the brain, messages the hypothalamus area to impulses to the pituitary gland, just below it at the top of the spine. The pituitary then stimulates the adrenal cortex with the adrenocorticotropic hormone (ACTH) to produce cortisol, commonly known as the stress hormone. The cortisol acts to keep both blood sugar and blood sugar high, assisting the body in its efforts to flee or cope with the perceived danger or another frightening event over a longer period of time. Other, non-life saving body processes are relegated to the back burner, such as digestion, immune response, growth, and regeneration.

What Are The Effects Of Short Term Stress On The Brain?

Short term stress causes the person experiencing it to feel anxious, distracted, irritable, and forgetful. Even one event triggers forgetfulness and tension. These effects may seem transient, but even when the perceived stress is infrequent, the brain still shows evidence of some loss of brain-cell communication in the areas of memory and learning.

Research indicates that a short-term stress may actually kill brain cells, stimulating them to the point where the brain creates fewer neurons in the hippocampus and destroys new ones as they are created. The speed with which the cells communicate with each other is also impaired despite the stress lasting a relatively short time.

What Are The Effects Of Long Term Or Chronic Stress On The Brain?

Researchers have found that chronic stress causes long-term or permanent changes in the brain's structure and its healthy functioning. Evidence indicates that stress that does not let up subjects the body to continuously high levels of cortisol which is damaging to brain and body.

Chronic stress appears to shrink the cells and total matter making up the brain, especially the hippocampus, which disrupts how this part of the brain reacts to current and future stressful events. Memory and emotions are regulated by the hippocampus, perhaps linking chronic stress to the demonstration of emotional disorders seen in individuals who report sustained stress or post-traumatic stress syndrome. The disruption of the operation of this part of the brain is likely behind some of the stressful reactions seen due to triggers that are not otherwise explainable as a cause of a stress response.

Stem cells are thought to be more likely to malfunction when under continual stress. The brain perceives itself to be in a continual state of "flight or flight," often out of proportion to the levels of stress a neutral person might report. The stem cells in a brain under extended stress are more likely to transform into cells called oligodendrocytes, which may be a predictor of later mental disorders.

Depression is one mental disorder now thought to have a direct connection with long-term, chronic stress. It's quite clear that chronic stress is related to depression. Studies of those diagnosed with depression reveal that a common modality among many is an over-release of cortisol into the bloodstream. Some researchers and clinical practitioners are now positing that the differences that are seen in serotonin and related neurotransmitters of people with depression may not be the cause of the disorder. Instead, the levels recorded are theorized to be a collateral effect of the changes in the brain functioning due to stress responses.

CHAPTER FIVE STRESS REDUCTION

- The deepest fear we have, 'the fear beneath all fears,' is the fear of not measuring up, the fear of judgment. It's this fear that creates the stress and depression of everyday life. - Tullian Tchividjian

When we are stressed it can affect our ability to think clearly and make good decisions. This can lead to things such as overeating and making silly mistakes with your work that you may not otherwise have made.

With this in mind it is not surprising that people look for ways to reduce their stress. We all find ourselves in stressful situations from time to time and we may feel as if there is nothing that can be done to improve the situation. However once your own stress is reduced then you may find that things are not as bad as they first seemed. You may want to try some of the things listed below next time you are feeling stressed as they have been shown to be successful for other people.

Take A Deep Breath

When you are feeling particularly stressed it can help if you take a few deep breaths. Concentrate on the breaths that you are taking as you breathe in and out for three or four times. When you are just thinking about breathing and nothing else then it can help to clear your mind of the things that have been causing you stress.

Go For A Walk

It can sometimes help to take yourself away from the situation that is causing you stress. Just taking a walk for ten minutes or so can really help you to clear your head. Exercise can also release endorphins which improve your mood and make things that would normally cause you stress seem as if they are not so bad.

Create A Support Network

If you have close friends or family then you may be able to talk to them when you find things are getting too much. They may be able to give you some advice about what you can do to try and deal with the situation. Even if they have no practical advice to offer then it can help just to have someone to talk to.

Take Some Time For You

Having some me time can really help make stressful situations seem easier to manage. Getting away from everything and just concentrating on things that make you happy can make it easier for you to deal with stressful situations when they do arise. Try and find some time for yourself a few times of week when you are able to put the things that are stressing you out to the back of your mind.

Find A New Hobby

If you have something that you enjoy doing outside of the things that cause your stress then this can help you deal with these situations. Finding a new hobby can also mean that you make new friends and extend your social circle. This can be very useful in improving your state of mind and making you feel more relaxed overall.

Accept That There Are Some Things That You Can't Change

There are certain things that may cause you stress that you can not do a lot about. When you accept that you are not able to change these things it can make it easier for you to rise above it. What you can do is concentrate on the things that you can change and take positive action to make these changes.

Appreciate What You Do Have

When we are feeling stressed it is all too easy to focus on the things that are going wrong and to forget about all the good things that we do have. However focusing on the positives in any situation can instantly make it seem less stressful. At the end of each day you could try and write down three things that went well during the day and that you are grateful for.

Set Yourself Some Challenges

When you challenge yourself to complete a task that you find daunting you will get a real sense of achievement when this task is completed. This can spur you on to try and push yourself further and before you know it you will be easing through things that would have previously made you stress. The key to this is to start out small and give yourself bigger challenges as you progress.

You may find that some of these strategies work better than others when you are trying to reduce your stress and that some may not even work at all. There are no rights and wrongs when it comes to the techniques that you should be using. As long as they work for you then that is the most important thing.

CHAPTER SIX TREATING STRESS

The Intense Burden of Psychological Stress

Stress is a very real medical problem. A lot of people still treat stress as being something that is outside the bounds of conventional medical science, partly because it is so conventional and partly due to dated beliefs about mental health conditions. Plenty of people still adhere to the idea that the mind and the body are separate, which is an old idea in Western thought in particular.

However, mental problems are physical problems. There is no separation. Stress can have a larger effect on the body than almost anything else. Being under constant stress is a risk factor for almost every long-term illness, from heart disease to high blood pressure. People who experience a lot of abuse, prejudice, or similar problems will often have more health problems as a matter of course. There is also the fact that stress has a way of exacerbating all diseases known to humankind. Stress is utterly disastrous from a medical perspective.

Of course, one of the worst parts of stress is the fact that it is so ubiquitous. Stress is an environmental factor. It is also the kind of environmental factor that shows up more than almost all others. Even people who are not burdened with histories of abuse, prejudice, and trauma can still get stressed out from almost everything in their normal lives.

Going to work can be stressful. Commuting to work is one of the most stressful things most middle-class and upper-class people do on a regular basis. People might love their families, but taking care of parents, children, spouses, and other loved ones can still be extremely stressful for even the most loving caregivers. Going to school can be stressful, particularly in this day and age. People all over the world will have a hard time avoiding stress, and it seems that climbing the economic ladder only does so much to reduce it. Treating stress as a health problem and real illness is even more important in an environment like this.

Lifestyle Treatments for Stress

One of the frustrating parts of stress is that it is so difficult to treat. Many researchers are well aware of the fact that stress is a hugely damaging risk factor in almost all diseases. In a lot of cases, they will simply recommend lifestyle changes for the treatment of stress.

A lot of researchers will suggest that people get more exercise as a way of coping with stress. Exercise is often touted as a cure for almost everything these days, of course. Some people do indeed find that exercise is useful in reducing stress. However, other people will only find that exercise augments stress, particularly given the culture surrounding exercise and the fact that exercise is connected to body-shaming issues today.

Some people also might be simply unable to exercise because of where they live and because of their budgets, which might not allow gym memberships. Lots of people would exercise if they could, but they can't find the time thanks to the suffocating work schedules that are causing them stress in the first place. Of course, there are other people who are stressing themselves out specifically in order to make sure that they can exercise regularly, so it's a complicated treatment method.

Some researchers will recommend other lifestyle changes in the treatment of stress. They might suggest that people change their diets, for instance. There are foods that are associated with negative mood swings. However, dietary changes can also only go so far. Many people will be able to improve their overall health with dietary changes, but the effects on stress will often be minor.

Researchers might suggest that people completely change their lifestyles, taking some more time for rest and relaxation and getting different jobs that are less stressful. However, this is only going to be an option for some people. For other people, this is just not going to work no matter how hard they try. In fact, trying to be less stressed can be a form of stress in its own right. Lifestyle changes will rarely be enough if the stress is actually caused by a mental illness.

Medications for Stress

In many cases, researchers will recommend medications. Stress is a byproduct of anxiety. Many anti-anxiety medications will be prescribed for the treatment of stress. These medications will have mixed results. For some people, they make all the difference in the world. For other people, finding a medication that works can more or less be a journey that they will complete with their doctors and psychiatrists.

The most common anti-depressants are known asselective serotonin reuptake inhibitors, or SSRI's. Popular SSRI's include Celexa, Prozac, Lexapro, Zoloft, and Paxil. Buspar is a popular medication that is used in the enhancement of serotonin. In the case of extreme stress and disorders like PTSD, doctors might prescribe Benzodiazepines. All of these different medications actually alter a person's brain chemistry in order to help them when it comes to the management of stress, increasing the neurological chemicals that are associated with happiness and decreasing the chemicals that are associated with stress in most cases.

However, it should be noted that there is nothing that is really marketed as 'stress medication.' People will be given medication to counteract anxiety, depression, or both. In some cases, people will be given multiple medication types. In a lot of cases, the medication is combined with behavioral therapy. Lots of people who experience chronic stress will go to therapists in order to manage their stress more effectively.

One of the tricky parts about prescribing medications for stress is the fact that there is a strong connection between stress and full-on mental illnesses. However, plenty of people do experience chronic stress without really being mentally ill in any real way. Then again, separating stress from mental illness can be difficult at the best of times. Stress is a symptom of a lot of mental illnesses. It is also a symptom of a lot of lifestyles.

?

? -Stress is the demon in our society, stalking the cities and the countryside, striking down young and old and growing in strength daily. -Srikumar Rao

-There's a lot of stress out there, and to handle it, you just need to believe in yourself; always go back to the person that you know you are, and don't let anybody tell you any different, because everyone's special and everyone's awesome. -McKayla Maroney

- If you laugh, you think, and you cry, that's a full day. That's a heck of a day. You do that seven days a week, you're going to have something special. - Jim Valvano

POST TRAUMATIC STRESS DISORDER

DEALING WITH PTSD

By.

Leo Hardy

CHAPTER ONE WHAT IS PTSD

-You have to understand that PTSD has to be an event that you experience, a very traumatic event. And actually, there is evidence that brain chemistry changes during this event in certain individuals where it's imprinted indelibly forever and there's an emotion associated with this which triggers the condition. - Dale Archer

Post-Traumatic Stress Disorder, or PTSD, is a term that has been an increasingly more talked about mental condition that most people immediately associate with the military. Although it is true, many men and women who currently serve, or have served in one of the branches of the military, suffer from this disorder to some degree or another. For years, PTSD wasn't fully understood or accepted as a true psychological disorder, not among the public, nor the psychological community. Many counselors or other medical professionals didn't know how, or with what to classify the behaviors associated with this psychiatric disorder in the years of the Vietnam War when veterans were returning home with clear, visible signs of post war trauma. It wasn't until the 1980's that the American Psychology Association finally accepted PTSD as a legitimate psychological diagnosis.

What is PTSD?

PTSD is classified as a mental condition that is brought on by terrifying events, either an event you experienced or witnessed. The event can trigger flashbacks, severe anxiety attacks, nightmares or night terror, along with the inability to control your thoughts about this event. Not every traumatic event brings on PTSD. Many people experience a traumatic or life altering event but with time, they are able to move past it in a healthy way by taking care of themselves and proper support. For others, the traumatic event only builds over time. There is no getting over it or moving forward. The symptoms that develop only intensify, prevent normal, everyday functioning and can last long periods of time - from months, to years.

Many men and women experience PTSD after deployments in the military. They are ones who are more prone to seeing and being a part of terrifying or life and mind altering events that will carry on well beyond the time the event is over. Although military events and situations are some of the most common causes of PTSD, but it can happen for any type of frightening experience; a home invasion, mental, physical or sexual abuse or rape cases. Sometimes it can be a horrific car accident that left you traumatized or any number of situations.

Signs of PTSD

Signs of PTSD vary in a wide range of emotions and behaviors. You may experience a few of the signs of PTSD, or all of the signs listed for PTSD, but any one of them is reason enough to seek treatment so that they do not disrupt your life, or the lives of those around you. Post Traumatic Stress Disorder can prevent itself in a number of ways and the signs shouldn't be ignored. Your friends and family may notice that you exhibit some of the following behavioral changes if you're suffering from PTSD:

• Feel irritated or start having outbursts
• Feel emotionally cut off or disconnected from others
• Feel upset or distraught by things that remind you of the traumatic event
• Always feel on-guard or on-edge, maybe constantly expecting something to happen
• Have trouble sleeping; insomnia or restlessness
• Have trouble concentrating and staying focused
• Feel jittery or nervous all the time. May get startled easily by things that used to not bother you
• Lose your drive for the things you once cared about. You're unmotivated or numb to life around you

• Have frequent, vivid nightmares or night terrors. May experience flashbacks to the terrifying events that took place and fear they will happen again

Reactions to PTSD

Post Traumatic Stress Disorder is not just about symptoms it inflicts on you, but it's about how you react to them. Your reactions to the symptoms can be life altering or disruptive to your well being and the lives of the ones you love and live with. Some of the reactions people may exhibit can be harmful to others and to themselves. It can be dangerous if certain behaviors begin to emerge and escalate. Some reactions people with PTSD are capable of expressing include:

• Stay to themselves. PTSD sufferers may begin to become recluse and not go out of the house much, socialize and become withdrawn

• Avoid situations, people and events that bring back memories or make them think of the terrifying event they experienced

• Have thoughts or plans to do harm to themselves or to other people

• Become a workaholic. Work extraordinarily long hours to help stay busy and avoid having to think about, or deal with their fears and the event

• Begin to rely on drugs or alcohol to numb yourself from reality and to cope

Treatments for PTSD

It's important that you seek treatment for your Post Traumatic Stress Disorder or help your loved one who you suspect is suffering from PTSD, to seek the professional help of counseling. There are different types of treatment that can be implemented in a PTSD program to help you learn to cope with your symptoms and get you back on track to living a peaceful, manageable and fulfilling life so that you aren't constantly battling the effects of the frightful event.

The most common ways PTSD counselors will work with you can include:

Treatments will typically include intense therapy. You will work with a counselor who specializes in PTSD treatment to help you understand your thoughts and reactions to your thoughts. He will help you identify your trigger sensors that set you off into a reactive state and help you learn coping mechanisms so that you can better deal with situations that would otherwise cripple you, physically, mentally and emotionally. You may be recommended to participate in group counseling sessions to work with other PTSD sufferer's and use each other's experiences as learning experiences.

Another form of treatment may include medication. There are multiple types of medications that can be used to help ease the effects that PTSD plays on the mind. Anti-anxiety medications can relax you and slow the over-thought process down that would normally send you into full panic mode. They keep you calm and rationale. Medications to help you sleep are important if you are having trouble night-after-night getting restful sleep. Lack of sleep is a core, mind and physical healer, and without it, your mind acts irrationally to the simplest of situations that make you uneasy. Your coping skills go way down without proper rest.

Bottom line

Most people who find a treatment plan they are happy with, work hard at it, and stick with it, will start to notice big improvements in their thought process and behaviors within just a few months. Don't let PTSD control you when you can gain control back of your life and learn to put the traumatic experience or event in its proper place - out of mind. And when it does come to mind, you have the tools to deal with it so that it no longer disrupts your life.

CHAPTER TWO PTSD IN CHILDREN

- You can't underestimate how traumatic divorce is for the children.-
Isla Fisher

Post-Traumatic Stress Disorder, or PTSD, is a disorder that is most commonly diagnosed in adults. However, it can affect anyone who has had a traumatic experience. Therefore, children who have had an experience related to death, serious injury or sexual abuse can experience PTSD. These children have had a situation involving these serious events happen to them directly or to one of their primary caregivers.

Some of the most common traumatic incidents that lead to PTSD in children include witnessing a situation where violence occurs or being the victim of physical violence; natural disaster, an accident, physical abuse or sexual abuse over time and even extreme neglect. These situations tend to lend themselves to issues that develop and increase over time, leading to a PTSD diagnosis.

For children under the age of six, memories or dreams of the event can continue to bother the victim. Also, the child can lose awareness of their current surroundings and have experiences as though they are back in the situation that caused them significant stress and fear.

Children can also have the following behaviors as such a traumatic experience:
- withdrawal from social experience
- loss of interest in play or interaction with peers
- avoidance of activities or locations that provide a reminder of the traumatic experience
- anger, irritability or severe temper tantrums
- increased vigilance and startle reaction
- restless sleep or problems falling asleep or staying asleep

- difficulty concentrating

The symptoms of PTSD can be present several months after the event occurred. This may seem like they are not connected. However, these are signs that children are not recovering from the event. Instead, they have developed PTSD as a result of the situation and their struggle to deal with it at their level of understanding. Stress occurs when the child continues to struggle to understand and move beyond the traumatic experience. Depression is a common result of this type of situation, and PTSD can occur because the child struggles emotionally to deal with the effects of the trauma.

The US Dept. of Veterans Affairs completed a study that found 3% to 15% of girls who experience trauma and 1% to 6% of boys who experience trauma experience PTSD (http://www.ptsd.va.gov/public/family/ptsd-children-adolescents.asp).

These children tend to suffer the most severe level of trauma and also to have the lowest levels of support at home. They also may have parents that are significantly impacted by the same traumatic event and may be dealing with PTSD as well.

While gender has been found to have an impact on the likelihood of suffering from PTSD, as girls are more likely to suffer PTSD than boys are, ethnicity has not been study enough to determine if certain ethnic groups are more likely to suffer PTSD than others.

The symptoms of PTSD can start to decrease and disappear altogether after a period of a few months. However, if the situation continues and children need some support and direction, Cognitive-Behavioral Therapy or CBT can be helpful. Trauma-Focused CBT allows the child to discuss their memories of the traumatic event and introduces methods to deal with stress and worry. The therapy works at the child's preferred pace, teaching them to relax when they think of the event and learn they do not need to be afraid of those memories, even though the memories can be painful.

Another method of treatment that can be used in schools is Psychological First Aid. This teaches children how to be calm and use problem-solving techniques. It also provides comfort and support.

Parents and caregivers who are concerned about the possibility of PTSD in children in their care should first learn about PTSD, then watch for symptoms. If the child exhibits these symptoms, you may need to reach out for professional assistance. Working with mental health professionals can make the process of helping a child recover go more smoothly.

CHAPTER THREE PTSD AND DIVORCE

The relationship between PTSD and divorce is complicated. For one thing, people who have PTSD are more likely to get divorced in the first place. The conditions associated with a bad or abusive marriage can cause PTSD. However, the stress of divorce itself can cause both clinical depression and PTSD. For the people who already have PTSD, this change can make their PTSD complex and even harder to treat.

Both spouses and children can get PTSD from a divorce. In fact, both spouses can get PTSD from the proceedings, including the spouse who was pushing the divorce in the first place. Marriage can provide a huge source of security for a lot of people both emotionally and financially. Having all of that ripped away right away can really cause a lot of pain and distress.

The stress of going through the divorce can cause PTSD. In some cases, just the simple act of being abandoned by someone else is going to be able to cause the PTSD. People who have a tremendous fear of abandonment are often going to specifically have PTSD. Some people who get divorced are going to relive the experience each and every single time that they try to form a new relationship with someone else. They're going to get the feeling that the new person is going to leave them and that they have to be on guard at all times.

This situation can be even more pronounced with the kids who are experiencing a parental divorce. They're going to be falling into a situation like this one very early in life. As such, it is going to have a huge effect on their development in general. This means that they are going to potentially face abandonment issues for a long period of time following the desertion of a parental figure. Many of the people who live in constant fear of a relationship falling apart are going to be the kinds of people who have experienced a parental divorce very early in life.

Most people will assume that this is only going to happen in the case of a formerly happy marriage. However, even in the case of an abusive marriage, people can be in situations in which they still mourn the loss of a marriage. In fact, abusive spouses can have a tremendous hold on their abused partners. Partners might be emotionally dependent on them in some way or another. This means that it is going to be traumatic to break a bond. Even when breaking a bond might be the healthiest thing to do, it can still be a traumatizing experience.

The fact that divorce can cause PTSD does not mean that people are morally obligated to stay in bad marriages. Childbirth can cause PTSD. A wide range of emotional circumstances can cause it. However, people need to be aware of the risks involved. They also need to know that divorce is never simple, emotionally or otherwise. Depression and stress can only be the beginning in some cases.

CHAPTER FOUR PTSD AND SUBSTANCE ABUSE

Millions of people worldwide are living with PTSD or Post- Traumatic Stress Disorder on a daily basis. PTSD is described as a mental health disorder, caused by the experience or observation of a traumatic event. The majority of the people who suffer from PTSD are unaware they have the disorder, and usually result in co- dependency of one or more drugs, including alcohol. When caregivers watch their loved ones go through one dramatic life crisis after another, the need to ease the hurt becomes a top priority. Pain is often relieved through a false sense of security, and drugs and alcohol are the main substances people turn to. This process is called "self- medication."Self-Medication of Drugs and Alcohol Brings About Feelings of Other Emotions When PTSD is present, so are feelings of anxiety, aggravation, and depression. While some people can overcome these feelings, others cannot, especially, when post- traumatic stress disorder develops. These symptoms do not go away without some type of intervention. In fact, these symptoms are normally present for months or years, before they are identified and treated. In today's society, people are faced with challenging situations that affect not only them but other members of the family, including their loved ones. Our military men and women are prime examples of how combat, can affect an entire family. Spouses and family members of military soldiers have to endure the pain of their loved ones screaming out at night, experiencing delusions, and sometimes trying to commit suicide. Before some people can get the help they need they turn to self-medication. Self- medication may consist of the use of illegal street drugs, prescription drugs, and alcohol. The purpose of using these drugs is to take away the pain and erase the memories of a bad experience. However, this is a temporary fix, not a solution, with dire consequences. Dual Diagnosis Often Accompany Post- Traumatic Stress Disorder

While post- traumatic stress might be the main culprit, there may be one or more underlying conditions that worsen PTSD. The brain is made up of many cells and synapses and chemicals. When the brain is abused through substance addiction, the chemical makeup of the brain changes. The feel-good chemical called endorphins that makes us happy is less present, due to the altering state of the brain. Drugs and alcohol can be described as mood- altering, or mood- enhancing drugs, which temporarily increase endorphin levels. Over an extended period of time, people who rely on these drugs to ease their pain will experience feelings of irritability, anxiety, and depression, as the drug wears off. When this happens, it is often the family members, friends, and loved ones that pick up the pieces, as the need for more drugs increase. Nevertheless, caregivers are affected by the actions they experience first- hand. They have to endure emotional stress, fear, anxiety, and sometimes thoughts of suicide. It is painful to watch someone you love go through one traumatic episode after another, knowing there is nothing you can do to help. It is often that feeling of hopelessness that drives people to drug and/or alcohol addiction and post- traumatic stress disorder.

CHAPTER FIVE PTSD IN THOSE WHO SERVE

*- Men and women who have served in harm's way experience higher
rates of divorce and suicide. Many battle the debilitating effects and
stigma associated with Post Traumatic Stress Disorder.- Ron Wyden*

It is a terrible thing when someone from a helping profession suffers
post traumatic stress disorder (PTSD). This state of mind might look
a lot to the onlooker like a depression, but the symptom profile for
this mental illness is often more complex. Those who serve in the
armed forces or law enforcement are often afflicted with PTSD.

PTSD is a condition that is triggered directly from stress. When
an individual suffers from an experience that is traumatic, especially
prolonged trauma, they may begin to display strange behaviors. The
individual might not appear to be particularly present in group set-
tings or one on one. It may seem like the patient is in another place
altogether. This is because essentially, that individual is. They are ro-
tating from the present to the past in their minds. It is like a tape that
plays over and over.

The reason that this happens is because the person cannot resolve
their past trauma. The sufferer did not come away from the experience whole, so to speak. There is a part of the soldier or law enforcement professional that seems to never have left the scene of the trauma.

That the person is stuck is an understatement. The patient is completely incapacitated by flashbacks of the incident or incidents. And
like a record that keeps playing on repeat, the same memories of the
trauma keep coming back. The funny thing though about it is that
the person feels like the hallucinations are real. When the memories come back, they are relived in vivid detail. Suddenly, the soldier
is crawling on the bedroom floor in the midst of gunfire. Ahead of
the soldier is the desert, vast and expansive, and the soldier must

figure out what to do. Usually the person just feels stuck because the individual is not happy with the reaction to everything the first time around. Maybe people died because of someone's inaction. Perhaps the intended action happened and a perpetrator did die. That doesn't mean that the service person felt any less shocked by the death. Sometimes even just the sheer violence of something will put the patient in perpetual fight or flight.

In our society today, all you have to do is turn on the television and you will see all of the crimes and hate that are going on in our world around us. There are so many violent topics of humans murdering each other, children bringing weapons to school, school shootings, hate crimes, and the list continues on. The individuals who watch this on the news are affected by it, and the individuals who are involved with these crimes, are affected by it even more. Most of them end up dealing with a lot of emotional issues after these events take place. Even though these types of situations are incredibly hard for anyone to go through, most people don't even realize the toll that these issues take on the police officers, EMT's, firefighters, and many other law enforcement officials. There are a lot of long term effects that can occur within these individuals in the law enforcement field, and there isn't many who realize just how much the these officials deal with emotionally. PTSD will end up occurring within the mind of these individuals, and they will end up having to deal with a lot of emotional trauma within themselves. There are many of these individuals who do not end up making it through this emotional disorder.

The shifts are long for law enforcement officers, the job is physically and emotionally dangerous, and the issues that they face are incredibly graphic, violent, and heart breaking. When a person is facing all of this on a daily basis, there are many different types of emotions and actions that can occur. There are so many law enforcement officials who have resorted to alcoholism, have ended up having heart attacks, developed depression, ended up getting divorced, resulting in domestic violence, and even suicide. There are so many of us who believe that officers are able to cope with all of the stress and violence that they occur with on a daily basis, however, this has been proven as false, and that it is exactly the opposite of what the media makes us believe about police officers. When a person has to deal with these issues on a daily basis, and face this type of violence, hate, and sadness, a person ends up not being able to cope with it all. This is when PTSD occurs within the individual, and they are not able to take any more of these daily stresses and they have completely lost who they are inside.

When it comes to PTSD and law enforcement, it is happening to more and more of these officials who are developing this condition from the type of situations that they are dealing with every day. An awareness of this issue is a way to help those who suffer from PTSD, and help to bring these issues to light. There are so many law enforcement officials who put their lives at risk every single day of their lives, and they endure a lot of emotional trauma from the job that they perform. PTSD is something that arises up inside of many of these police officers, and they need help just like anyone else who endures this type of issue.

When the symptoms of PTSD arise, they look a lot like depression because often the sufferer is unwilling to share the reality of what he/she is experiencing. The sufferers can fear that they will look crazy and be locked up forever. There is a bit of paranoia involved too because there is still a stigma against mental health, so a person might not be guaranteed to be met with a warm reception if that individual does ask for help. Also, the trauma that the patient experienced has affected the overall view of mankind. There might be quite a bit of darkness in the mind which basically just painted all humans with a black brush. The hopelessness of that state just means that people will not reach out for support, nor do they believe anything will get better. In their mind, it is all bad.

To reach out to people who might be suffering can be daunting. However, people need others to talk to them about reality. Otherwise, they will completely escape into fantasy and avoidance. Mental illnesses and conditions rarely resolve themselves on their own. Patients need the proactive involvement of professionals, colleagues, and loved ones surrounding them to help them realize that they might be ill. And that illness is an alright state to be in because there is always the hope of recovery. There are many treatments available for PTSD, but a sufferer will not experience them if the person does not recognize what is causing their PTSD and depression.

Many people will never have to go through what soldiers do on the battlefield, or what a law enforcement professional encounters when in the thick of crime and vice. Most people avoid those situations in life completely because they understand that their psyche will not cope well with dangerous situations. That is why these professionals are relied upon so much to come in and fill in the gap. However, not everyone can cope with the aftermath of what is experienced in a traumatic event. The event can catch a person off guard and forever change the person. Or the person might be alright for years and then suddenly reach a breaking point or encounter a situation that is just too much for even that trained professional to handle.

There is a light at the end of the tunnel. Even if a person does not know how to help a sufferer, the individual can confidently say that. There are new treatments for PTSD that arise every day, and so the person has a lot of options to choose from. This is better than years ago when the individual might have only been presented with medication that had a lot of side effects. Also, there are talk therapy groups and individual counseling sessions that most of these workplaces pay for because they are that concerned with their employees' mental health.

Taking the time out to be aware that those in traumatic situations might not always cope the best in the aftermath is important. It can help others be more appreciative of the service that special forces do on their behalf. It can also help in interactions with people they might know. They need to be sensitive but realistic. It is not fair to assume that others can compensate for abnormal behavior, so everyone needs to be on the page that a realistic approach is best. Let them know that they might not be seeing things clearly at the moment and might need to take a break to heal. Let them know that if they need to talk, people are available.

PTSD is like any other mental illness. It disrupts the lives and service of important professionals, but is a condition which can be resolved with the help of supportive workplaces, home life, psychologists, and psychiatrists. It may take some team work, but PTSD victims that are treated can emerge even stronger than before.

CHAPTER SIX TREATING PTSD

When a person has been through a traumatic event they may experience the trauma well after the event has ended. Horrifying memories can be triggered by a number of different things. They may cause the body to go into panic mode and active the natural flight or fight response. When a person is suffering from post traumatic stress disorder also known as PTSD there is no easy way to overcome this. With the proper treatment a person can learn how to manage their PTSD and take back their life.

Recognize the Signs

The first step to treating PTSD is to recognize the signs of this condition. If a person keeps experiencing the trauma event has feeling of nervousness or fear when they are talking about this event is one of the tell tale signs of PTSD. Being startled and scared of loud noises can be a sign of PTSD. A person may have this condition if they lose interest in the future. They may have feelings of hopelessness and may no longer have an interest in once enjoyable activities. If a person has these signs they may be suffering from PTSD and should be aware of the different treatments that are available to them.

Admit the Feelings

A person should monitor how often they have feelings of fear or flashbacks. These feelings can be kept in a journal. In addition to how they are feeling they should write down what trigger the flashbacks, their physical location, and what they experience in the presence. This will make a person aware of any events that are bringing back this traumatic experience. While they are doing this a person should also monitor their feelings of avoidance. This means they are blocking out parts of the traumatic experience from their memory. This can be forgetting the events or purposely making them go away. A person may also refuse to go to a place that reminds them of this event. Feelings of emotional numbness are often common. They shut out event positive experiences and seemed to have forgotten how to feel joy.

There are several forms of therapy that can be used to help a person with post traumatic stress disorder.

Cognitive Therapy

This type of therapy will allow a person to talk to a trained professional about their feelings and patterns that keep bring back the traumatic memories. They will be able to talk about feelings of the trauma or the traumatic event occurring again and what they can do to overcome this feeling of constant fear and depression.

Exposure Therapy

This is used with cognitive therapy so that a person can learn some new behaviors in addition with their self expression. This is a behavioral therapy that will allow a person to work on changing their behavior. They will face situations that have been using the trauma and the memories that are associated with this event. This therapy can be helpful for people that are having flashbacks. If a person is experiencing nightmares they can also benefit from this type of therapy. They will revisit the setting in their mind and learn how to reenter the situation but this time they are in control of the situation.

EMDR Therapy

This therapy will use eye movement to help desensitize a person and help them reprocess their memory. They will help a person reprocess the information that is associated with the traumatic event and learn how to handle the memories associated with the experience. This therapy will use a series of guided eye movement The eye movement will be used to help a person process their traumatic memories and change the way that they react to these memories. This therapy needs to be done with a professional therapist and they will determine if additional techniques are going to be needed.

Medications

While people may can help a person control their symptoms of PTSD. Medication should be used in combination with therapies and recording the memories and symptoms.

Antidepressants

These medications can help a person with PTSD. Antidepressants can be used to help with the symptoms of depression as well as anxiety. There are a number of antidepressants that can be prescribed by a qualified doctor in addition to therapy. Medications including Paxil and Zoloft have been approved by the Food and Drug Administration for use to help treat PTSD and help to ease the symptoms.

Anti Anxiety Medication

These drugs can help a person with anxiety and some problems that have been related with PTSD. Some of these medications may lead to abuse so many people are only on them for a short period of time.

Prazosin

These medications can help people that are seeking therapy while they are dealing with issues of insomnia and reoccurring nightmares. These medications include prazosin can help a person suppress their nightmares and be able to get some sleep. A person once again needs to take this medication with some form of therapy so they can get to the root of their problem. Be sure to tell the doctor about any unpleasant side effects that are happening in addition with the medication.

Addressing Symptoms

A person will learn how to recognize their symptoms and address them. That way if a person is out in public or around others they do not have to go into panic mode. They will be able to know what is happening and will take steps to bring them back to the present time.

When a person is suffering from PTSD they need to seek treatment. A person should not have to live with the fear and the depression. When a person experiences a traumatic event and is suffering from PTSD they need to seek help. They need to monitor their symptoms and when the fear and anxiety kicks in. A person can also start a therapy program to help them get past the issues they are experiencing. PTSD can take over a person's life but with the proper therapy and treatment they can get over this condition and take back control of their life.